Pamela Rushby

The Hero's Journey

Text: Pamela Rushby
Publishers: Tania Mazzeo and Eliza Webb
Series consultant: Amanda Sutera
Hands on Heads Consulting
Editor: Kirstie Innes-Will
Project editors: Jarrah Moore and Annabel Smith
Designer: Leigh Ashforth
Project designer: Danielle Maccarone
Permissions researcher: Lumina Datamatics
Production controller: Renee Tome

Acknowledgements
We would like to thank the following for permission to reproduce copyright material:

p. 4: History and Art Collection/Alamy Stock Photo; p. 5: Pictorial Press Ltd/Alamy Stock Photo; p. 6 (top): LANDMARK MEDIA/Alamy Stock Photo, (bottom): Pictorial Press Ltd/Alamy Stock Photo; p. 7 (top): WARNER BROS MGM/Alamy Stock Photo, (bottom), p. 3: FlixPix/Alamy Stock Photo; p. 8 (top): FlixPix/Alamy Stock Photo, (bottom): LANDMARK MEDIA/Alamy Stock Photo; p. 9 (top): United Archives GmbH/Alamy Stock Photo, (bottom): Everett Collection Inc/Alamy Stock Photo; p. 10: Pictorial Press Ltd/Alamy Stock Photo; p. 11, Title page: LANDMARK MEDIA/Alamy Stock Photo; p. 12 (top): LANDMARK MEDIA/Alamy Stock Photo, (bottom): Allstar Picture Library Limited./Alamy Stock Photo; p. 13: Cinematic/Alamy Stock Photo; p. 14: Collection Christophel/Alamy Stock Photo; p. 15 (top): Szabolcs Magyar/Alamy Stock Photo, (bottom): cineclassico/Alamy Stock Photo; p. 16 (top): Warner Bros./Photofest, (bottom): United Archives GmbH/Alamy Stock Photo; p. 17 (top): United Archives GmbH/Alamy Stock Photo, (bottom): TCD/Alamy Stock Photo; p. 18 (top): Warner Bros/Everett Collection Inc/Alamy Stock Photo, (bottom): Entertainment Pictures/Alamy Stock Photo; p. 19, Index p. 32: Chris/Adobe Stock Photos;p. 20 (top): TCD/Alamy Stock Photo, (bottom): United Archives GmbH/Alamy Stock Photo; p. 21: New Line Cinema/Everett Collection Inc/Alamy Stock Photo; p. 22 (top): Photo 12/Alamy Stock Photo, (bottom): United Archives GmbH/Alamy Stock Photo; p. 23: LANDMARK MEDIA/Alamy Stock Photo; p. 24 (top): Lionsgate/Photofest, (bottom): Murray Close/PhotoFest; p. 25: © Lionsgate Photographer/Murray Close/Phtotofest; p. 26: Lionsgate/Photofest; p. 27 (top): FlixPix/Alamy Stock Photo, (bottom): Lionsgate/Photofest; p. 28: Moviestore Collection Ltd/Alamy Stock Photo; Front cover, p. 29: iStock.com/E+/Koh Sze Kiat; p. 30 (bottom): iStock.com/SeventyFour.

Every effort has been made to trace and acknowledge copyright. However, if any infringement has occurred, the publishers tender their apologies and invite the copyright holders to contact them.

NovaStar

ISBN 978 0 17 033481 5

Cengage Learning Australia
Level 5, 80 Dorcas Street
Southbank VIC 3006 Australia
Phone: 1300 790 853
Email: aust.nelsonprimary@cengage.com

For learning solutions, visit **cengage.com.au**

Printed in China by 1010 Printing International Ltd
1 2 3 4 5 6 7 29 28 27 26 25

Nelson acknowledges the Traditional Owners and Custodians of the lands of all First Nations Peoples. We pay respect to Elders past and present, and extend that respect to all First Nations Peoples today.

CONTENTS

WHAT IS THE HERO'S JOURNEY?

You've probably seen a movie or two with a storyline that goes something like this: The main character's ordinary life is suddenly changed by a "call to adventure" – an important reason to leave their ordinary life behind. The hero is often **reluctant** at first, but something changes their mind and they respond to the call. They enter a new world and meet friends – and enemies. They come across danger. They struggle to defeat enemies and evil, and solve tricky problems. Finally, the hero is successful and returns home **victorious**, their life changed forever.

Tales with a storyline like this are very, very old. Many of the tales and **legends** of ancient Egypt, Greece, Rome and Britain have this **structure**.

The ancient Greek story *The Odyssey* that tells of the long sea voyage of Odysseus is a classic example of the Hero's Journey.

This storyline is so common that it has a name of its own: the Hero's Journey. The journey is a **quest** the hero goes on. The quest storyline is often used in movies. The Hero's Journey provided the structure for the popular 1939 movie *The Wizard of Oz* and more recent movies such as *The Hunger Games* series. The journey can be very lengthy and complicated, such as in *The Lord of the Rings* series, the *Harry Potter* series and the *Star Wars* series.

Let's look at each stage of the Hero's Journey over the page and how it appears in *The Wizard of Oz*.

Dorothy is the hero of *The Wizard of Oz*. Her friends are the Scarecrow, the Tin Man and the Cowardly Lion.

The Stages of the Hero's Journey

The stage of the Hero's Journey	What happens?	How it appears in *The Wizard of Oz*
THE ORDINARY WORLD	Life is ordinary.	Dorothy lives on a farm in Kansas, USA, with her aunt and uncle. It's so dull her life there is shown without any colour.
THE CALL TO ADVENTURE	Then adventure calls.	An unpleasant neighbour threatens to take away Dorothy's dog, Toto.
REFUSING THE CALL TO ADVENTURE	Often the hero is not keen on going on the journey, so they refuse at first.	Dorothy runs away with Toto to keep the dog safe – but she turns back.
A CHANGE OF MIND	Something changes their mind.	Dorothy has no choice but to answer the call to adventure: a tornado whips her up and drops her (and Toto) in the Land of Oz.
CROSSING THE THRESHOLD	The hero crosses a **threshold** and enters a new world.	Oz is full of colour – and strange people.
MEETING THE MENTOR	The journey begins. The hero may meet a wise helper, or **mentor**.	The Good Witch, Glinda, gives Dorothy special ruby slippers, and tells her that if she wants to go home she must follow the Yellow Brick Road and ask the powerful Wizard of Oz for help.

The stage of the Hero's Journey	What happens?	How it appears in *The Wizard of Oz*
MEETING FRIENDS — AND ENEMIES	Often, the hero meets friends along the way, and makes enemies.	Dorothy befriends the Scarecrow, the Tin Man and the Cowardly Lion. Her enemy, the Wicked Witch of the West, pursues them because she wants the ruby slippers.
THE ORDEAL	The hero bravely faces an **ordeal** – challenges, tests and danger. Things don't go smoothly. But the hero wins in the end.	The Wicked Witch corners Dorothy and her friends and tries to burn the Scarecrow. But Dorothy throws a bucket of water, which hits the Witch – and she melts. Dorothy then meets the Wizard of Oz and finds he's not wise and powerful at all. He can't help her. How will she get home?
THE RETURN	The hero returns.	Glinda explains that the ruby slippers can help Dorothy get home. Dorothy and Toto return home to Kansas safely. 
THE REWARD	The hero gains something valuable.	Dorothy has grown up a lot and learnt how much she loves her home and family.

A FAMILIAR STRUCTURE

Think about favourite childhood fairy tales, such as Goldilocks and the Three Bears, Red Riding Hood and Cinderella. Do they follow this structure?

The movie examples in this book follow the Hero's Journey structure – but sometimes there are interesting changes. See if you can spot them.

STAR WARS: EPISODE IV — A NEW HOPE

Luke Skywalker is the hero in *Star Wars: Episode IV — A New Hope*. This is his journey.

The Ordinary World

Luke Skywalker lives a dull life with his aunt and uncle on a farm on a desert planet.

Luke comes from the planet Tatooine.

The Call to Adventure

Luke buys two new droids, or hi-tech robots, called R2-D2 and C-3PO. He finds a mysterious message hidden in R2-D2: Princess Leia of the planet Alderaan is calling for help from someone called Obi-Wan Kenobi.

Princess Leia asks for help in a special message.

Meeting the Mentor

Luke follows R2-D2 and meets up with wise old Obi-Wan Kenobi. Obi-Wan used to be a Jedi, a legendary knight who can use the powerful Force. Long ago, he fought against one of the leaders of the Galactic Empire, the evil Darth Vader. Obi-Wan asks Luke to join him on his mission and offers to teach Luke the ways of the Jedi.

Obi-Wan Kenobi was once a Jedi.

Refusing the Call to Adventure

Luke turns down the offer. He's needed on the farm. But when he returns home, he finds that his aunt and uncle have been killed by Galactic Empire Stormtroopers. The Stormtroopers were looking for R2-D2 and C-3PO.

The Stormtroopers wear armour that covers their faces.

A Change of Mind

Luke now agrees to accept the quest to help Princess Leia, Obi-Wan Kenobi and the **rebels**, who are fighting against Darth Vader and the Galactic Empire.

Crossing the Threshold

Luke journeys with Obi-Wan Kenobi to a new world of strange creatures, life forms from distant planets.

Meeting Friends

Luke meets two space adventurers, Han Solo and Chewbacca, and Obi-Wan hires them to help him and Luke.

On their way to Princess Leia's planet, Obi-Wan Kenobi teaches Luke to fight with a lightsaber, a powerful Jedi weapon.

Han Solo and Chewbacca transport Luke and Obi-Wan in Han's ship, the Millennium Falcon.

Luke learns how to use a lightsaber.

The Ordeal

The planet Alderaan has been destroyed by the Galactic Empire's huge planet-sized ship, the Death Star. Luke overcomes many dangers to meet Princess Leia. Together they escape from the Death Star. Luke joins the rebel fleet as a pilot, and finally the Death Star is destroyed. But Obi-Wan Kenobi is killed by Darth Vader.

The rebel fleet attack the Death Star.

Obi-Wan Kenobi fights Darth Vader with a lightsaber.

The Reward

The rebels have won – for now. Leia awards Luke and his companions medals for their heroic actions.

Luke does not return to his ordinary world. He remains with the **rebellion**. There will be more for him to do.

As princess, Leia presents Luke and Han with their medals.

HIDDEN INSPIRATION

The story of *Star Wars* was inspired by a 1958 Japanese movie called *The Hidden Fortress*, which also followed the structure of the Hero's Journey.

HARRY POTTER AND THE PHILOSOPHER'S STONE

Harry Potter and the Philosopher's Stone is the first in a series of movies about a young boy who learns he is a wizard on his eleventh birthday.

The Ordinary World

When Harry is just a baby, Harry Potter's parents are killed by the evil wizard Lord Voldemort. Harry lives with his aunt, uncle and cousin: the Dursleys. They are unkind to him; they make him sleep in a cupboard under the stairs. The Dursleys have no magical powers and think that Harry is strange because he can do things like speak to snakes.

Harry Potter has a magical ability to talk to snakes.

The Call to Adventure

Magical messenger owls begin to deliver letters inviting Harry to attend Hogwarts School of Witchcraft and Wizardry. The Dursleys hide these letters, so Harry can't read them. But finally, one of these letters gets through to Harry, delivered by Hagrid, a kindly half-giant who works at Hogwarts.

Hagrid looks after the grounds at Hogwarts.

Refusing the Call to Adventure and A Change of Mind

The Dursleys have refused the call for Harry, by hiding the letters. When Harry finds out, he is keen to leave the Dursleys and go to Hogwarts. He accepts the call.

When Harry doesn't respond to the first letter, more and more magical letters arrive at the Dursleys' home.

Meeting the Mentor

Hagrid is the first mentor Harry meets. He tells Harry that Harry is actually a wizard and he is very special. As a baby, he survived an attack by Lord Voldemort. Hagrid takes Harry away to the wizarding world and explains lots of things to him. Later, Harry meets another mentor, Professor Dumbledore, the Hogwarts headmaster.

Professor Dumbledore

Crossing the Threshold

In the magical world of Diagon Alley, Harry gets his school supplies, including a magic wand. He visits a bank run by goblins. Harry then boards the special train to Hogwarts.

Hogwarts is a magical place where the staircases move by themselves.

Meeting Friends — and Enemies

Harry meets friends Hermione and Ron, as well as those he believes are enemies: Draco Malfoy and Professor Snape.

Harry, Ron and Hermione become close friends.

Draco Malfoy (centre) is a bully who often tries to pick on Harry and his friends.

The Ordeal

Hogwarts school can be a dangerous place. Harry has to struggle against **trolls**, a three-headed dog and a magical mirror that can swallow a person's **soul**. Even the magical sport of Quidditch, played by students on flying broomsticks, can be life-threatening. Harry, Hermione and Ron find a mystery they want to solve. To do this, they must pass three tests.

In one of their ordeals, Harry, Hermione and Ron have to play a dangerous game of "wizard chess".

Finally, Harry has to battle Lord Voldemort, who everyone thought was dead. He faces Voldemort in combat but is tempted to join Voldemort's forces by Voldemort saying he can bring Harry's parents back to life. Harry resists, and Voldemort is defeated – for now.

Lord Voldemort is Harry Potter's enemy.

The Reward

The wizarding world is free of Voldemort – for a while. Harry and his friends win the House Cup for their bravery.

The Return

At the end of the school year, Harry must return to the Dursleys. But as soon as school starts again, he knows he can come back to his new home at Hogwarts.

The Hogwarts Express will bring Harry back to school each year.

SEVEN BOOKS, EIGHT MOVIES

There are seven books in the *Harry Potter* series. But there are so many adventures in the seventh book, *Harry Potter and the Deathly Hallows,* that the book was made into two full-length movies.

THE LORD OF THE RINGS: THE FELLOWSHIP OF THE RING

The Lord of the Rings: The Fellowship of the Ring is an adventure film set in a fantasy world. It tells the story of Frodo Baggins.

The Ordinary World

Frodo is a hobbit, one of a **race** of small people. He lives a happy, peaceful life in the Shire, with his uncle Bilbo and his friends Sam, Merry and Pippin. A wizard called Gandalf arrives to celebrate Bilbo's birthday. There's a fun party.

Bilbo's party is a cheerful event, but Bilbo has a secret.

The Call to Adventure and Meeting the Mentor

During the party, Bilbo leaves the Shire. He gives Frodo the powerful and mysterious One Ring, which Bilbo has held for many years. Gandalf, now acting as a mentor, tells Frodo that the Ring has the power to cover the whole world with darkness and evil. He asks Frodo to take the Ring on a dangerous journey, so it can be destroyed. Gandalf leaves to get more help for Frodo's journey, arranging to meet him again soon.

Gandalf asks Frodo to help him destroy the Ring.

Refusing the Call to Adventure

Frodo doesn't believe a simple hobbit like himself can succeed in this quest. He doesn't want to go.

A Change of Mind and Crossing the Threshold

Frodo finally agrees to deliver the Ring to Gandalf at Bree, a nearby village. He and his friends Sam, Merry and Pippin leave the Shire (for the first time ever) and head to Bree.

The world outside the Shire is a dangerous place for Frodo and his hobbit friends.

Meeting Friends — and Enemies

The hobbits are chased by Ringwraiths, deadly servants of the Ring under the control of the evil Lord Sauron. The hobbits hide, and survive. At Bree, they meet Gandalf and a new friend, Strider, a mysterious traveller.

Frodo is wounded by the Ringwraiths and taken to the elves, who heal him. Frodo recovers and then volunteers to take the Ring to the fires of Mount Doom to destroy it. The Fellowship of the Ring is formed to help Frodo on his quest. The eight members of the Fellowship include elves, dwarves, hobbits and humans.

Elves, dwarves, humans and hobbits join together in the Fellowship of the Ring.

The Ordeal

The Fellowship is forced into the dangerous and dark Mines of Moria. They are chased by evil creatures including **orcs**, a cave troll and a fearsome monster called a Balrog. They believe that the Balrog has killed Gandalf. At last, they reach the safety of the elves' home of Lothlórien.

Orcs are frightening creatures.

The Reward

The Fellowship is rewarded for their bravery by Galadriel, an elf queen, with special gifts. But Frodo must continue the journey to destroy the Ring.

The Return

There is no return to the Shire yet, because the quest isn't complete. The Fellowship leave Lothlórien. One of the members of the Fellowship attempts to take the Ring and seize its power for himself, but Frodo escapes with the Ring. Frodo realises he must go on alone, but his loyal friend Sam refuses to leave him. Together they go on towards Mount Doom. Finally, in the third movie, they are **triumphant**, destroying the Ring, and they return home.

Frodo holds the Ring above the fires of Mount Doom.

BOOKS FROM THE 1930s

The *Lord of the Rings* story was first published as three books in the 1930s and 1940s. The three movies were made in the early 2000s, and the story of the hero Frodo continues to be very popular today.

THE HUNGER GAMES

RELEASED 2012

The hero of *The Hunger Games* is a young girl called Katniss Everdeen.

The Ordinary World

Katniss lives in District 12 of the **dystopian** world of Panem. Following a war, the districts are under the harsh control of The Capitol, a hi-tech city where the rich and powerful live. District 12 is very poor. Katniss hunts to keep her family from starving.

Katniss is an excellent hunter.

The Call to Adventure

Every year, each district is forced to send two young people to The Capitol to take part in the Hunger Games. This is an event shown on TV where **contestants**, called "tributes", fight each other to stay alive. Only one tribute survives the Games each year and "wins". This year, Katniss's younger sister is selected to compete. Katniss volunteers to take her place.

Katniss volunteers as tribute so that her little sister doesn't have to compete.

Refusing the Call to Adventure and A Change of Mind

Nobody in District 12 wants to compete in the Hunger Games, but Katniss only has two choices: she can let her little sister die, or she can save her. Katniss answers the call.

Meeting the Mentor

Katniss is introduced to her mentor: Haymitch, a previous survivor/winner of the Games. He is not the usual wise mentor – he has been badly affected by taking part in the Games. But he knows how they work.

Haymitch acts as Katniss's mentor.

Crossing the Threshold

On the journey to The Capitol, Katniss enters a world completely different to what she knows. It's a world of technology and **luxurious** living.

The luxury of The Capitol is very different from the life Katniss has known so far.

The Ordeal

Katniss has to train and gain experience before the Games begin, and attract **sponsors** who will help her during the Games. She has support from her preparation team and District 12's other tribute, Peeta.

During the Games, Katniss has to battle with other tributes who are trying to kill her, as well as the many dangers of the Games environment. She is injured, but finally she and Peeta are the final two survivors. Only one of them can win ... but Katniss and Peeta decide to break the rules. They threaten to eat poisonous berries at the same time, leaving the Games with no winner.

Only one person can win the Hunger Games.

Katniss and Peeta have to train hard before the Games.

TO PROTECT OR SAVE!

Often the hero of the story decides to go on the adventure to protect or save a loved one. If Katniss's sister hadn't been chosen as tribute, Katniss would never have gone on this journey and had this adventure.

The Reward

The Capitol changes the rules and declares two winners. Katniss and Peeta become popular heroes.

The Return

Katniss and Peeta have won, so they can return home to District 12. This should be the start of a new life for them, and new hope for the poorer districts. But it isn't a happy ending. The Capitol's president, Coriolanus Snow, doesn't like being **outwitted** by tributes. He wants revenge. Katniss will need to go on a new Hero's Journey in the next *Hunger Games* movie.

Coriolanus Snow is Katniss's enemy in the next films in the *Hunger Games* series.

WHY IS THE HERO'S JOURNEY STRUCTURE SO POPULAR?

Movies with a Hero's Journey take viewers out of their everyday lives. Certainly they start in the everyday – but then the hero is challenged to go on a journey and extraordinary things happen. Audiences like to see the wonderful and frightening places, different people and strange creatures the hero finds on the way.

Along the journey, the hero's courage inspires us. As we watch, we can forget the problems of ordinary life, as the dangers the hero faces make real-life issues seem small and unimportant. The hero's bravery in dark times gives us hope. They **persevere**, do their best and work with others. And we realise it's possible for monsters to be defeated, for dragons to be tamed and for good to overcome evil. The hero is triumphant.

THE HERO'S JOURNEY IN REAL LIFE

There's nothing new in the structure of good stories. Storylines that include the Hero's Journey have entertained and fascinated people in tales and legends from ancient times until today.

You can use the structure of the Hero's Journey to become a hero yourself. Think of your own life as a story: every day, every week, every month you set out on adventures, both large and small. You are the hero of your own stories. You face challenges such as starting at a new school, trying out for a sporting team, getting an assignment in on time, making new friends, or maybe something as big as changes within your family.

Do you refuse the call to adventure– or stride out to take on what might be a new world? On the journey, you may learn new skills from others. You may have to face enemies and challenges. But heroes face their enemies and challenges – and overcome them. And they return triumphant.

Just like Luke Skywalker, Harry Potter, Frodo Baggins and Katniss Everdeen – you too can be a hero!

YOUR OWN HERO'S JOURNEY!

You can use this structure if you're writing your own quest story. Try using the table on pages 6 and 7 to write your own story about a Hero's Journey.

Glossary

contestants (*noun*)	people who participate in a competition or contest
dystopian (*adjective*)	describing a society where most people live unhappy or even miserable lives
legends (*noun*)	stories handed down from early times
luxurious (*adjective*)	very comfortable and expensive
mentor (*noun*)	a wise and trusted teacher
orcs (*noun*)	ugly, mythical creatures
ordeal (*noun*)	a test or trial that is difficult to go through
outwitted (*verb*)	tricked or defeated by a clever act
persevere (*verb*)	to keep going despite difficulties
quest (*noun*)	a journey to find or accomplish something
race (*noun*)	a group of people who share many of the same physical characteristics
rebellion (*noun*)	a fight or uprising against a government
rebels (*noun*)	people who rise up or fight against their government
reluctant (*adjective*)	afraid to do something
soul (*noun*)	the spiritual part of a person that some people believe lives on after the body dies
sponsors (*noun*)	people who pay the cost of something
structure (*noun*)	a whole made up of various parts
threshold (*noun*)	what you step across when you enter a room; a place of beginning or entering
triumphant (*adjective*)	victorious or successful
trolls (*noun*)	mythical large, dangerous creatures from Northern European folklore
victorious (*noun*)	having won a fight or battle

Index